A Word on Taproot Press

Like *Plague Clothes*, Taproot Press was a project born in Lockdown, but the idea was conceived as early as the summer of 2019, when we first began discussing its direction and identity. Initial plans had been put on hold, but when Robert Alan Jamieson was faced with the problem of how to circulate poems written during the Covid-19 pandemic, a unique opportunity emerged to bring the press into being.

    A taproot grows from the radicle of the seed and is the primary root from which other roots sprout. It is the link between the underground and the over-ground; between the visible and invisible. Culturally, it is that which connects the local with the global, the micro with the macro. For Scotland, a nation that has long identified itself internationally, this is particularly resonant. As the late Gavin Wallace wrote: 'Every voyage inward is a voyage out: with a vitality and vigour unprecedented since the twentieth-century literary renaissance, post-devolution Scottish writing is being inwardly nourished by the deep, outward-reaching international taproots of Scottish culture.' It is in this spirit that Taproot Press will operate, publishing contemporary, radical voices emerging from both Scotland and the rest of the world. Recent events have reaffirmed the importance of the written word in connecting us across all kinds of divisions. This is the moment – when other lines of communications are severed, when contact is restricted – that language must be recovered as a tool for forging community, not fragmenting it, for challenging systems of oppression, not enforcing them. Taproot Press will offer a platform for those who wish to do this.

    By supporting Robert Alan Jamieson's *Plague Clothes*, you are directly contributing to the establishment of Taproot Press. It is because of the kindness shown by each of the two hundred-plus subscribers that we will be able to publish future titles, to continue to grow and voyage out.

    Thank you.

Daniela Silva & Patrick Jamieson
19.6.2020

Plague Clothes is published by Taproot Press in an edition of 500, of which the first 250 copies are numbered and signed by the author for the subscribers who helped make it a reality.

To Daniela Silva, Eleanor Jamieson-Chang, Jennie Renton, Miranda Pearson, and especially Patrick Jamieson, who have all helped to make this book during Lockdown; and via these efforts, to Taproot Press, may it flourish for many long years in the love-stream; and lastly, to Finlay Jamieson-Silva, Aeira Terayama-Jamieson, and all the other small children across the world in whose future, I hope, Covid-19 will be an episode in history that people once learned from, so to make that future safer and kinder than it would otherwise have been.

Plague Clothes

Poems from the Covid-recovery love-stream

17th April–17th May 2020

ROBERT ALAN JAMIESON

First published by Taproot Press 2020

ISBN: 978-1-8380800-0-6

The author's right to be identified as author of this book under the Copyright, Designs and Patents Act 1988 has been asserted.

Printed and bound by Bell & Bain Ltd., Glasgow.

Typeset in 11 point Garamond by Main Point Books, Edinburgh

Text and photographs © Robert Alan Jamieson 2020

Contents

Prelude	14
I reach the garden at last	18
I am losing the habit of speech	19
I sense the sadness	20
I am among the old and vulnerable	21
I despair of our Leaders	25
I don't know whether	26
I have no poetry	27
I begin an argument with myself	28
I don't care too much for money	29
I see the Leader in a flattering new guise	30
I interrogate the front door	31
I want to feel the weather	32
I dream the emotional range	33
I consider going feral	37
I grow curious about the World	39
I wonder what fake news to believe	40
I don't know where the ejector seat button is	41
I claim the Noble prize for economics	43
I read *The Ministry of Sanctioned Walking Advice to Old & Vulnerable Pedestrians*	46
I have been here before	54

I read the guidance on Auto-lalia	55
I wonder whether Mondays are the saddest of days	56
In the silence, I hear many things	57
I blame the weather gods	58
I hear 'Take Peace'	59
I listen as the Great Leader issues a Great Decree	60
I await renovation	62
I fear the full flower moon	65
I remember the dead on the anniversary of victory	66
I look upon a distant coastline	67
I didn't want to know little Nico's story but then	70
I find it hard to speak of the ineffable	72
I respond to a friend's request for my postcode	73
I call it now what it is, a culling	74
I don't know WTF to say	75
I will survive (won't I?) O Leader?	76
I must rise	77
I see an old man breaking quarantine and smile	78
I learn of the Lives of Others	80
I see a man well camouflaged by stone	82
I think the Police may be bored	84
I video-conference with my Selves	87
I write a letter of resignation to the Future	89
I prepare the Pyre	90
Dear Subscribers	93

These poems were written between the 17th of April and the 16th of May, 2020. The sequence began with a few tentative lines written in a sick bed, after I'd already been ill for a month with a virus that matched Covid-19 symptoms.

Writing them became a daily mental exercise, an attempt to regain sharpness, corollary to the physical exercise I began to take from that first poem on, up and down the river walk that leads from my home to the sea at Cramond, when I'd meditate on my mood, perhaps some news story, or something I saw as I walked – or rather trudged like a very old and vulnerable person. The poems were written quickly on returning home, directly into Facebook status updates, and not really revisited afterwards.

Though the process of recovery was slow, in the spirit of instant response which marked the writing, this collection is rapidly produced through the most immediate channel, and dedicated to all my friends near and far, whose responses to the poems as I posted them became a vital communication with the world during Lockdown. It was a part of what I came to think of as, not livestreams, but a 'love-stream' between us all, those sharing their thoughts and ideas, their art and craft, and those responding.

Robert Alan Jamieson
17.5.2020

We lost us for a while.

Until we were ill
we didn't know how sick our world was.

Until all was silent
we didn't know how noise polluted.

Until the hospitals were full
we didn't know how brave the staff are.

Until the animals came to town
we thought them dead, or they'd deserted us.

Until we saw nobody
we didn't know the ones we'd miss.

Some we'll miss forever.

Prelude

25th March – I find myself doing things more slowly these shut-in days. Time isn't something to save any longer, by hurrying the opening of the cat food, or working out the simplest way of doing the most chores, or juggling time to meet, or move between those meetings. Instead, time is more a thing to spend, in going down the little side-track I thought led nowhere, in lingering and looking, reflecting.

1st April – First walk since I fell ill. Not a marathon, though it felt a bit like one coming back, but I went down the river walk to Cramond and along the foreshore to the shuttered Boardwalk cafe, then back through the woods and the village to the Falls Cafe – which is, sadly, up for sale. All the public car parks are shut, and it's 'Residents Only' access. Yet there's a few people out and about – I met neighbours and we chatted at a broom's length. Slowly, some fitness is returning. I couldn't have done that a couple of days ago.

2nd April – May have overdone the walk yesterday – feel very tired today, as if I've aged the last couple of weeks to become one of the old folk, sitting by the fireside, reminiscing.

9th April – 28 days since I first felt the unexpected cough and went into retreat, and today is the first when I can honestly say I feel well. Not I'm a little better or I'm getting there, based on hopeful micro-calibrations in the wild fluctuation of the infection, whatever it was (note the past tense) – but actually possessed of a desire to do things, to go out and see people, and to talk agai –
oh, wait.

13th April – Made it to the foreshore and back with some ease this morning. Didn't dare go so far as the first time. But not even the river walk is without a reminder of the times we live in. Graffiti on the Salvesen Steps: COVID19

16th April – Oh so quiet down the river walk today – a snell wind coming up the gorge from the North Sea seemed to keep folk away. All the various boats are still high and dry at Cramond – so I got a surprise when I thought I heard the wind catch a sail repeatedly behind me. Then, from the hidden water below the harbour wall, a swan swept up beside me and beat its way out into the headwind, towards the tide-locked island. Just a little 'Sibelian'.

17th April – I was just thinking, all these live-streams, these 'sharings' here online, collectively are a kind of love-stream between us all.

Plague Clothes

17.4.20

I reach the garden at last

A month of pestilence indoors
and the vegetable plot ignored is
full of tiny blue flowers, all waving and smiling,

signing sarcastically

>   forget-me-not
>   forget-me-not

>   forget-me-not

21.4.2020

I am losing the habit of speech

Language itself grows strange.
I forget the names of all I knew.
Colour, shape and texture blend.

Those things there, what are they called?
Those people, what is it that they do?

How do those little words go
sense to make situations of?

Soon, I will only meow
     or bark
     or quack.

My tweets will all be bird-like.

22.4.2020

I sense the sadness

New-leaf trees can almost mask
loss that lingers, a mist among them.

They do not care a twig
what humans carry round within
those stupid little heads –

news of illness, death, the ache
of separation, all irrelevant.

Birds fly in, and birds fly out.
The higher skies are silent.

Below, the humans wander,
avoiding touch as if it were
forbidden in this slow dance.

They smile and nod, turn their faces
to the trees that sway, regardless.

But I sense their sadness.

23.4.2020

I am among the old and vulnerable

The Government has issued information
relating to my current circumstance.
Therefore, it must be carefully considered,
by a chap of what is now a certain vintage.

That I am quite old, I cannot
sensibly deny,

cut open, cracked and broken, confused, and blind
to some degree. What I thought I once knew
no longer holds. The world grows strange,
full of things I can't be bothered learning,
like the latest acronym, or what *Love Island* is.

I forget my many passwords
endlessly.

But aren't we all so vulnerable – say, to a plum stone lodged?
Regardless of our years, it takes no time to choke,
to slip beneath the wheel of that oncoming bus, or fall
and bash our heads as we exit the shower, half-awake.
Gone, out like a light, this *us*, this *we*, the *I*,

yet aren't some still catching buses, eating plums,
at ninety-three?

I'm not convinced you've researched me,
the suffering endured, or – so far – dodged.
I fear, alone at home here, sick, that I remain
another small statistic you don't know.

I do take care. And so should you.

24.4.2020

I despair of our Leaders

Personally, he is not a man to mince words.
Personally, he would wear neither mask nor gloves.

Personally, he is sure it is an enemy hoax.
Personally, he would not think twice about shaking hands.

Personally, he believes it will be gone miraculously by Easter.
Personally, he may have infected his pregnant lover.

Personally, he suspects it is a foreign plot.
Personally, he is sure that if enough people die, all will be well.

Personally, he would happily try the untested drug, why not?
Personally, he is certain the great people of his country will prevail.

Personally, he would shrink to fight the genius bug, *mano a mano*.
Personally, he is ready to take one for the team.

Personally, he thinks sick bodies should be blasted with light.
Personally, he is recovering well on his country estate.

Personally, he's injecting disinfectant into his lungs.
Personally, he hasn't worked for quite a while.

They talk, our leaders, on the phone, reassuring people –
what terrific guys, doing such great jobs, true friends.

    We're in good hands.

24.4.2020

I don't know whether

to laugh or cry into my whisky tonight?
On the one hand, that would dilute it,

while the other could cause
inadvertent inhalation,

      possibly choking.

But one way or another, I need it.
The human world is so, so

        benighted.

And it isn't even six yet.

25.4.2020

I have no poetry

I have porridge.

All too grey,
too confused,
this morning.

The horizon
between sense
and information gone,

lost in mist,
last night's dream escape
itself forgotten.

Yesterday's sarcasm
was never truly funny,
just wild defence, against folly.

I pour on a little milk,
watch as it pools.

Can I eat this simple prose?
Can I thole this tasteless morsel?

25.4.2020

I begin an argument with myself

It's so easy to start. Frustration bursts out
in curses, everything's fragile in this silence,
and there are so many things to be irritated by
with no one around to complain to.

Inside, I break my glasses, turning over in the bed.
I set a plastic carton on the still-hot stovetop.
Outside, litter trails, left by the daily picnickers.
I blame them, but forget to bring a bin-bag.

Yet, sometimes the river gods do intervene,
restoring equilibrium. Today I heard a voice,
a woman keening by the weir, to a loud
accompanying rush of water, falling.

Seven perfect notes repeated, seven times over.
No words, but both a melody and meaning.
She left the sound to echo, where I picked it up, as I
half-blindly mopped sour milk, and then forgave me.

26.4.2020

I don't care too much for money

Must be six weeks since it jangled in my pocket,
since coins were important – or indeed notes.

That community cafe where they didn't take cards,
I think, when I drove home from the festival of poets.

It can't buy me breath, nor health, nor touch now.
Not even my supplies from the local Tesco –

a dead commodity nobody wants, if it can't
pay the cashier for a bottle of Prosecco.

I dandle none, dander to the shore, no where
to go and nothing there to buy when I arrive.

Other matters matter more now – new-born
values that are somehow very old and wise,

precious as those four tiny ducklings that
repay my real expense of energy in walking

by two trembling minutes of splash-play –
instinctive, feathery balls, together frolicking.

Live, little ones. Avoid the crows.

Flourish.

27.4.2020

I see the Leader in a flattering new guise

Thing with ironic sarcasm is,
not everybody gets it.

But now I see how clever
the Great Leader is with wordplay,
a lot of things fit into place.

    Like MAGA.

So smart, it should be
on a hat

    made in China.

27.4.2020

I interrogate the front door

I deconstruct constituent parts,
mentally separate hinges from frame,
panels, lock and handles, but your sum
is greater than all this: your border post.

    You do not answer.

You always swung so smoothly, fit so well.
I've never told you I admire that,
how you perform your simple function
without a squeaked complaint, or hesitation.

    I hope you know

if ever you've refused the task I asked,
it was because I'd heaped up coats on you
or left my boots to block your route –
it was always my fault, never yours.

    I hope you know that?

Now you keep me in, you keep others out.
Two-faced, but not duplicitous.
I wish you'd answer when I ask, who's there?
Say, *only me, relax, I'm here for you.*

    Why so still, silent one?

27.4.2020

I want to feel the weather

Indoor surfaces reflect the same dull scene repeated.
Even the not-so-polished, or decontaminated.

Screens. Dusty Glass. Streaky Windows. Cracked
Mirror. Dull Lamp. Varnished Picture.

Ceramic Glaze. Gloss Covers. Tin Foil.
Laminate. Porcelain.

Wood and paint.
Plaster.
And plastic, always plastic.

All pass the dwindling
light between them till it fades.

But no hint of weather touches me.
The sun doesn't reach, even at sunset.

Just the numb, seeping inwards slowly through
the skin, the eyes, the disengaging brain,

as I press my nose against the flat cold pane
and cough. Inside here, breath is haar – rain, a tear.

28.4.2020

I dream the emotional range

Every night,
I'm out there, a
desperado.

Landscape
I thought I knew
reveals new swamps.

Horse has no name,
Just an old song
we sing sometimes.

Her voice is not
what I expect
but a mermaid's.

She steps warily.
By moon or star
I have to trust

she knows the way
to morning, east
is her bearing.

Four hooves plod on,
slow percussion,
soporific.

Fragments of light
appear, but they
won't coalesce.

Dawn's indistinct.
The words all come
from different songs.

Exhausted, I
awake to salve
the sores of day.

28.4.2020

I consider going feral

The garden had seemed a place of shame,
overgrown with a sick spring idleness.

The sign I made last year, old already,
stonework, pocked with isles of moss.

The pond, a pool of rotting leaves and twigs,
the fancy shop-bought windbreak, broken.

The lawn, a sunny dandelion thick-pile,
the cloche, an ocean of forget-me-not.

Yet the cherry tree still drops white blossom,
the lilac bloom still casts an aromatic spell.

I check the chaos, find beauty firmly rooted,
smiling as the bees fulfil their careful duties.

Two tabbies prowl through long grass, catching
nothing but the wind from a butterfly's wing.

All kinds of creatures, most tinier than human
eyes can spot, creep in this miniature universe.

The soil is seething, a healthy mass of friable life.
Seeds sprout, unsown. I feel somewhat unsettled

to be so little missed. This summer, maybe I should
just observe, let all unfold, this constant wilding?

Our straight lines, close-crop hedges, all that mowing,
the wish for outside to be neat like inside, seem wrong.

Let me roam around the long grass, as the cats are,
roll about in sunshine. I know I'll heal much faster.

28.4.2020

I grow curious about the World

It's six weeks since I last switched TV on.
Six weeks since I ordered anything.

Tonight, I anticipate a curry from Miraj,
and who knows, maybe I can stomach TV too?

What's going on in there?
Are there still soap operas?

Is there *Celebrity Lockdown*?
Does *Big Brother* broadcast every night?

Are there invented sports scores,
like Oceaniania 2, Mesopotamia 4?

> I love Big Brother.
> I must be getting well.

29.4.2020

I wonder what fake news to believe

It's said the Leaders disagreed on Easter Exit Strategy.
Allegedly, one listened to his faith advisors – Just pray

and the miracle will happen. Our great and godly country
will re-emerge reborn, and open on Easter Sunday.

Allegedly, the other took counsel from his tactical guru –
It's not enough to hope, he heard, you basically have to do

the things that make the symbol work for you.

Actually, come Easter Sunday, in the former country,
still too sick to open,
despite its Leader's thoughts and prayers,
nothing marvellous did happen.

But in the latter, a shock-haired stocky hero staggered
from his labyrinthine struggle with a killer-viral mugger.

AN EASTER MIRACLE !

tabloids announced,
in full-cap swagger

Allegedly.

29.4.2020

I don't know where the ejector seat button is

Not that I'm anybody's martini
but this has shaken me.

I realise the truisms, how tenuous our
grip on life is, the dangers we face daily –

and I'm no special agent, with or without
those fancy gadgets at the ready.

I realise, too, how fast we're ageing,
in living through epochal change,

as if while time has halted socially,
it has privately accelerated.

This before-and-after marks
another phase, another stage,

for sure, but we're not there yet –
the after bit. Right now, I'm lost

at home without a mission
or a map. No sports or car.

I can't see anywhere to go. Like
somebody slammed the brakes

and now it's all slo-mo, a free-fall
arcing by in milli-milliseconds

towards the foggy windshield.
The airbag hasn't inflated.

This ain't no movie.

30.4.2020

I claim the Noble prize for economics

Okay, I know I'm not a financial doctor,
but I got a you-know-what – a billfold.
and I know that when I got no money,
I gotta find a way to get me more.

Maybe a bank loan, maybe a credit card.

But what you got here is like a massive hole
in your pocket where the billfold falls through.
Like there's hardly anybody gettin paid now,
and nobody's gettin rich except morticians.

So first we gotta plug that hole.

No point puttin new money into that old pocket
unless we make that leaky hole good first.
Cept of course it's not real money, not like gold,
just numbers on a banksheet, lines of credit.

So we need to think smarter, right?

It's nothin a sharpie can't fix. So you just take
your latest statement and find the balance,
you know, what's left when all's gone out and in,
and what you gotta do is shift the zero.

Make that zero a million – see, that's better?

It's got a name, it's called recalibration, right?
Now I know what you're all gonna say. If
everybody adds a million to their balance, won't
that make billionaires comparatively less rich?

Ah, but here's the beauty – they get a million too!

1-2.5.2020

I read *The Ministry of Sanctioned Walking Advice to Old & Vulnerable Pedestrians*

KNOW YOUR CYCLISTS !

A Walker's Guide

In these times of Lockdown where the limited sanctioned walking areas are shared with cyclists, the Ministry of Sanctioned Walking seeks to advise old and vulnerable pedestrians on the many types of cyclists they are liable to encounter today.

As you are no doubt aware, cyclist numbers have increased dramatically in recent times as, like other wildlife, they have moved in to occupy spaces previously filled with cars. Indeed, Lockdown is the perfect time to begin to get to know these varied creatures, and the subspecies you are likely to encounter.

This knowledge has a practical use as well, as your understanding of their behavioural patterns will help you to avoid contact, including collisions, in these times where exercise space is so limited, and social distancing so necessary.

Know Your Cyclists 1:

The Alpha

These are mostly male, though not always. Sometimes they move so fast it's impossible to tell, and sometimes the observer feels only a passing breeze before catching the briefest glimpse as they dart past.

They purr with precision engineering and complex gears, and normally wear black as opposed to coloured Lycra.

They give no warning cry when approaching, but their remarkable ability to manoeuvre at pace through small gaps between pedestrians makes collision unlikely.

They have no interest in you but are closely monitoring speed and heart-rate and various other bodily matters. Learn to recognise the distinctive purr, hold to your course, and you should be safe.

Alphas are the ninjas of cycling and little is known about their real lives, or even whether they exist. However, the Government advice is that you should feel safe around them and walk steady.

Make no sudden move. They bear you no ill will.

Know Your Cyclists 2:

The Beta

This subspecies shares many of the characteristics of the Alpha, but for various reasons can be more dangerous.

They generally possess the capability for Alpha-like cycling in terms of their mount, but in most cases their performance is less physical and more symbolic.

Their plumage is always highly coloured, and gadgety.

What makes them dangerous is: a) their own disappointment in not actually being Alpha, which can lead them to blame pedestrians for getting in the way and spoiling what otherwise would definitely have been their best time; and b) a need to be noticed which, in effect, slows their progress; and c) frustration at having spent large amounts of money on something which they cannot be best at.

As a consequence, these creatures may attempt unsafe manoeuvres, or even orchestrate collisions, for which you will be blamed.

Their distinctive cry is a loud 'Fuckyou', repeated as often as necessary. Be wary. One saving grace, however, is the tendency of many Beta to ring bells loudly as they approach, warning you to move aside. Do so.

These are not to be tangled with. They are looking to vent. As a stupid old person, you are an ideal target.

Know Your Cyclists 3:

The Gamma

These are probably the most common and the most charming of the various subspecies, a hugely varied group, as are their mounts. Some have out-dated models which regularly break down, others are mounted on brand new deliveries which they are not quite in control of as yet. Nonetheless, the flocks move as one.

In terms of plumage, Lycra is not uncommon amongst those Gamma who aspire to be Beta yet are restrained by their group loyalty, but often the lesser examples go about in any old thing they picked up on the way out the door.

Whereas the Alpha is entirely solitary, and the Beta moves mostly in highly competitive twos or threes, Gammas gather in larger multi-generational family flocks which move at a leisurely pace, for the most part blending well with pedestrians, often stopping to talk or take selfies. However, they tend to be so absorbed in each other and flock-like that they take over the entire footpath, and force the pedestrian to take evasive action.

They do not observe social-distancing, as it is foreign to their nature. Therefore, despite their appealing calls (e.g. 'Smile!'; 'Cheese!'; 'Slow doon, wull ye, Schumacher!') and fascinatingly varied appearance, it is best to avoid close contact. Their very unpredictability makes them a possible threat. Smile, but don't get talking. They like old people, as they always remind them of dead Nan or Grandpa. They will surround you quickly and squabbles readily break out. How do you know what colour of eyes Nan had? Do not engage, or look shifty.

Know Your Cyclists 4:

The Delta

These creatures, like the Epsilon which we will encounter in the final section, often lack the distinctive cap, or helmet, of the classes previously discussed.

They move slowly, indeed spend almost as much time pushing their mount as riding it, sometimes due to mechanical failure or flat tyres, but such is their happy disposition that they do not seem to care.

They are easily distracted by any little feature of interest, and spend much time admiring butterflies, bees or birds.

They tend to move in couples, possibly courting, and cycling itself seems of secondary importance.

Their call is a cooing, not unlike that of the turtle dove, with a repeated 'Loook'.

Plumage is entirely Lycra free, yet may be quite stylish, if a part of the courtship ritual.

They pose little danger to the elderly pedestrian, but will object fiercely should they suspect any such passer-by of spying on them, so if you do possess binoculars it is best to conceal these till you have navigated a safe social distance past them.

Never tut-tut.

Know Your Cyclists 5:

The Epsilon

Finally, we come to the least common and most dangerous of the various subspecies. Like the harmless Delta, the Epsilon often has no cap, or helmet – unless worn backwards – but unlike the Delta this class is almost exclusively male, and do not seem to reach the adult stage, except in a few rare cases. Their mounts are called BMX, mini-sized, and appear as if they have been ridden continuously since fledging.

Plumage is usually dark, though ostentatiously labelled, the exception being their seasonal sporting attire which is brightly coloured and speaks of a secret code of tribal belonging which old people cannot understand. They rarely flock in large number, but groups of up to six or seven are occasionally encountered. They are not malicious unless provoked, because they all have Nans or Grandpas, but have no concept of safety and are continually attempting dangerous tricks to impress each other.

Whilst they do not achieve the sustained velocities of Alpha or Beta, they can sprint very quickly and suddenly for short distances. They are completely oblivious to the existence of other creatures beyond their social grouping. Their cry is often hard to distinguish, and endlessly varied, but notes of 'yafuckindancerya' or 'yacuntya' do sometimes emerge.

Avoid the Epsilon at all costs – unless you address them, they do not know you exist, and if you should suddenly shatter their illusion they can turn nasty, small though they may be. Unsheath walking stick swords, if you have them.

SUMMARY

In conclusion, the Minister wishes to advise caution at all times, and urges you to absorb the scientific data offered here, as the current phenomenon of a rise in cyclist numbers may indeed turn out to be the new normal, in which case you may have to walk on the restricted sanctioned paths in the midst of them for the foreseeable future. Until the Ministry is satisfied the that rise in cyclist numbers is stable and manageable, we must take every precaution.

If the problem worsens, it may be necessary to reserve the hour of 8–9 a.m. for your exclusive use.

3.5.2020

I have been here before

A time when
you aren't allowed
to go to any shop
beyond the local store
for bare essentials

and if you want
anything else
you have to order
and wait forever
for delivery.

        Childhood,
        it was called.

4.5.2020

I read the guidance on Auto-lalia

When giving yourself a good talking to,
try to emphasise the good.
You don't want to be your own worst critic.

Listen to yourself talk. You may be sick and tired
of the sound of your own voice,
but you may have something to bring to the table.

Try to be respectful at all times, if possible.
Never curse your own stupidity.
Let yourself finish whatever you want to say

before replying to any points you may have raised.
Never correct your own grammar.
Nobody likes an inner pedant, least of all you.

Whatever speech impediments you may display,
just you let them pass. Stammering
is perfectly understandable, under such duress.

If outdoors, use headphones so you hear yourself,
and other people will ignore you,
assuming you're merely on the phone to a friend,

which in a way you are, or should be. But
if you simply won't shut up, do call 111
and ask to speak to someone.

4.5.2020

I wonder whether Mondays are the saddest of days

When we expect to get out and about,
to be doing, however much we don't want to?

Now it seems to be the day
when the old weekly life's most absent.

That Monday Morning Feeling
had a certain positive charge,

an energy now missing, maybe
a sense of being involved?

Never thought I'd say
I miss Monday.

5.5.2020

In the silence, I hear many things

In the absence,
I discovered the forgotten,
and in the timelessness,
I found a little soul.

I'd thought it a myth,
or mystery without solution,
but there it was, all this time,
something transcendental,
beyond consciousness.

It had no meaning.
It had no message.
It had no question.

I would have brought it home
to care for it, had it not
seemed quite content right there,
out in the timeless wilderness.

It wants no feeding.
It wants no rest.
It wants no comfort.

It simply is.
It must be.

6.5.2020

I blame the weather gods

It's done its best to make our sanctioned walks
more tolerable, providing ample opportunity
to get a little sunshine in.

I've read that April was the sunniest here,
the driest, since 1929, with ninety extra hours
of precious vitamin D.

At least, I'd like to think it intentionally kind.
If not, if it was taunting us, with unenjoyable joys,
old TSE was right,

     and the lilac bloom is dying
     for the want of water.

6.5.2020

I hear 'Take Peace'

That's what the old folk used to say,
such a familiar idiom, I had to check
to be sure it wasn't English.

Said if somebody was agitated, anxious
or fidgety, maybe pacing about –
someone like me, maybe.

I hear their voices in my head now,
saying, 'Boy, tak paes, sit still.'
It was a wisdom

I didn't appreciate then.
Now I get it

    I do.

7.5.2020

I listen as the Great Leader issues a Great Decree

Many more must die, he tells them,
many more must yet be sacrificed.
Brave warriors all, required now, to
appease the monster at the door.

And so they come forward, those
warriors – or rather, they stay
where they are, because they can't
escape as others quickly do.

As the Great Leader orders his aide
to open the gates, and admit the foe,
they stay, those warriors, with their
carers, as the enemy approaches:

Gramps with his hearing aid switched off;
Great-Aunt Lily, snug in her bath chair;
Cousin Geoff with his compromised
immune-system; and thousands like them.

The Great Leader calls his favorite TV host,
to be reassured he'd come over presidential,
and smugly retreats to the executive suite
to watch the reruns of his speech. Then,

bored, he flicks his phone onto his own
favorite clip – that one of him felling
that wrestler with a single fake blow,
having snuck up on him from behind.

He laughs. Time for the golf simulator.
So many courses to choose from, but
he selects one that he owns. He swings
his driver, sends the ball into the water.

Delete. Another drive: this time, sand trap.
Delete. And on, till the eighth attempt
sits pretty, and he mounts his simulated
buggy, to steer off down his fake fairway.

It will all be so much easier soon, when
he's playing for real again, and his guys
are out there with spare balls, placing them
right where they should land, each shot,

he always gets the best lies then. A mashie
swings. Damn those bone-spurs, FORE!

7.5.2020

I await renovation

I'm feeling strange in strange ways I've never felt before. Sick, locked in, repressed at a social level, obviously – but somehow other than those words convey.

Today I saw another of the many signs, where the walk to Cramond Isle begins, and realised, while reading it, a substantial part of who I am is currently

Closed Until Further Notice

7.5.2020

I fear the full flower moon

It pulls hard tonight, tilting me out
of shape, drawing the liquid self
away from solid ground.

Escape, it says – fly!
You can if you try!

But matters are heavy, their weight
holds me down, in place, frightened
of unknown heights.

I may howl a bit later
as I can't go that far,

or pick lilac bloom before dark falls,
inhale their scent all night,
a sublunary drift.

It is a kind of flight,
the unconscious state.

8.5.2020

I remember the dead on the anniversary of victory

Those who died on all sides.
Those who have died to date.

Those who have no one to mourn them.
Those who have gravestones and flowers.

I do not project a number that is acceptable,
that number is total – in time, the sum of all of us.

But I mourn all those who died for lack of care,
whose lives were considered collateral.

I mourn all those who died from want of food
or water, across the fence from plenty.

Weep for those we loved, for those we knew,
who were our people, and were strange to others,

yes – but aren't there tears enough for all,
our strangers too, and human folly?

8.5.2020

I look upon a distant coastline

Not so long ago, or was it long (how
do we measure these things now?)

I stood across there, on that shore,
and looked at where I'm standing, here.

It was so close, then, an hour away at most.
Now it's months from here at least,

and I'm like a child, gazing, fascinated
by the thought of all the people gazing back –

how do they spend their days?
Do they walk the beach as I do,

feeling child-like themselves,
imagining the city with its spires

and galleries, its shops, and try to guess
when they'll wander through it next?

What wonder this suspense stores up
for us – for some day soon, some future

yet unknown or undefined, a time
when we, like children, can explore

a world we'll rediscover – is immense.
A foreign kingdom calls to me,

an hour or months away – Fife.

9.5.2020

I didn't want to know little Nico's story but then

sometimes, no matter how much you may try to go faster – or stop just to let them get ahead of you – it's impossible to avoid the shouters. Little Nico was slow, he was looking around, going too near the harbour, picking the dandelions, hitting bollards with an outsize stick – and worst of all, scuffing his trainers.

Dad's were immaculate – in fact, all of Dad was polished, a regular guy in the best of condition, clothes all pressed, and the other, smart son tripped along, measuring his stride to avoid being different. Mum was lagging, not so fit but hotter than she wanted to be. Nico was playing.

I did my best to lose them, but it seemed that I was fated to learn their family dynamic, going home. Once, I even ducked into the undergrowth to try to shut the shouting out. I trembled then for little Nico, when he'd get home, shut in, and the damage to his trainers was inspected.

I stopped to let them move ahead – I watched the ducklings –but not so far along the path, I caught up to them, sitting, all gathered in a hunch beside a fallen tree trunk. Dad was shouting 'Look!', 'Look!' and, fearing what I'd see, I circled round, what seemed two metres, as I passed.

And then, from out of the father's hands, a painted lady flew right past my head. I smiled at them, Dad smiled at me, good son and mother too. Little Nico laughed out loud, and hugged himself.

'Butterfly! he shouted, happily. And scuffed his trainers.

9.5.2020

I find it hard to speak of the ineffable

Or that liminal space I'm held in
between now and then, and maybe –
battles cessated in some fragile truce.

Released from service, I spend hours
surfing memory that isn't so much past
as where we are, or riding high

on hope that's no doubt ill-advised,
and certainly ill-founded, of
a permanent peace.

There is no retreat,
no surrendering.
There is no avoiding

whatever is coming in
that thunderous advance.
It must break around us –

that wave, that deafening
soporific draught, sweeping
the sleeper away.

Close your eyes, let it break.
You can't prevent it.
You are an obstacle

it does not see.

10.5.2020

I respond to a friend's request for my postcode

My address is the whole of my world,
now centred on the edge of the edge
of our Old World. If that still exists.

There may be nothing beyond this now,
not even dragons, I wouldn't know.

Or maybe a matrix of actors, recorded,
pretending they're politicians, and the
journalists who interview them,

playing on loop. I wouldn't know,
I can't see farther than the door.

My mind turned inward quite a while
ago, and isn't interested. It won't allow
the outside in, so inside out is it.

I'm here, though, all the same,
still somewhere down the lane.

    Still sane? I wouldn't know.

10.5.2020

I call it now what it is, a culling

A culling of the old.
A culling of the sick.
A culling of the poor,

a culling of the weak.

I saw no change of heart,
just camouflage and bluster
over insincerity, personal
drama to distract.

Aim stated: immunity.

You heard it too.

13.5.2020

I don't know WTF to say

Largely, I have restrained myself –
for a while I was too ill to do otherwise.

But now, now that I'm a Lert and fully functional,
I have no option but to ask of the honourable member
for Uxbridge

>   FFS,
>   WTF,
>   WTAF
>
>   d'ye think yer daein,
>
>   yaprickya?
>
>   WTAF,
>   FFS?
>
>   W. T. A. F.

13.5.2020

I will survive (won't I?) O Leader?

Perhaps …
if the Gods will it,
and don't demand the ultimate …

    you know

Assuming that …
you are not amongst the groups
which are earmarked for …

    you know

If circumstances …
at this point in time our models
… if you'll bear with me … suggest …

    you know.

However, as the man in the street might say
I wouldn't go the whole … you know … Gloria
Gaynor. However, my message to you is this.
Rich people are becoming less so.
The bulldog spirit is rather dilute.
We must … perhaps. However …
and … ah … yes. Perhaps.

    Yes, perhaps not.

    Jolly Good.

14.5.2020

I must rise

This dream is sometimes very real – it
even has food, and hunger, and bodily
functions. Weather and long naps.

Illness, boredom. Sneezing and coughing,
laughing and crying. Walks. Hearing voices,
thinking you're probably going crazy.

You'd almost believe you're actually awake

except it's really too surreal, and you've
lost all power of movement, bar to
stretch yourself out, on the divan,

turning yet another blurry page.
In the dream, you can't but wonder,
has the snooze button stuck?

    Where is the dawn?

14.5.2020

I see an old man breaking quarantine and smile

Ex-Isle, his boat's called.
A bonnie wee Westerly
but seen better days.

She'd been out of the water
since autumn and longs to
be lying at anchor again,

tired of waiting for the old grey
man from the island to come,
to take her out to sea again.

He never says much,
lets the wee radio play
music from far off.

She knows him, though –
his movement, his care.
She trusts his touch.

He misses her greatly as well,
has dreams of sneaking down,
polishing brightwork, caulking.

From the top of the house,
he can just see her mast below –
horizontal, still, so distant, yet

signalling come, where are you?
Tomorrow he'd risk it, he'd visit.

14.5.2020

I learn of the Lives of Others

    So glad we've got the chance
    to talk alone. Chin-chin.

It was all rather decadent, wasn't it?
Those air miles, the restaurants,
shopping malls, the bars and clubs?

All those theatres and brothels.
The spas and tanning suites,
and those endless, endless cafes.

    It couldn't go on. Except, of course
    for those in the Party.

Who did those people think they were,
squeezing onto budget jets for two weeks of sun?
The Kardashians? Trumps? Ridiculous. You'd laugh
if it didn't make you money.

All that choice, all that fakery.
They loved it, then. The posing,
the selfies, look-at-me,
FOMO teasing. All so very
very vulgar. But,
lucrative.

A kind of mad consumption
in the old sense – a rampant disease,
a debilitation of the soul by
over-exposure to a fatal spore,
desire.

Except for those in the Party.
We don't make a fuss.
We don't need masks.
We are tested daily.

    Another drink?

We can have whatever we want.

    If you hear of anything,
    you'll let the Bureau know,
    of course.

15.5.2020

I see a man well camouflaged by stone

For four days now, a man has faced a wall –
each time I've passed, he's been there,
as if engaged upon some mammoth task

of strange religious observance.
And perhaps he is – maybe the bucket
doesn't just have mortar in there?

And maybe the wall is more than stone
to him, maybe it is home, his fort,
his castled keep against the virus?

Who knows? He never turns to see
who passes, the cyclists or the runners,
or just old dawdlers like me. He never speaks,

but seems to want to be invisible, to find
security in camouflage, and most don't seem
to see him where he lurks, so barely moving.

Maybe he feels too guilty, being there, working
outside in a public space, at a time like this?
That might be the very reason only the

faintest scrapes of trowel escape his silence.
Today, he'd reached the point where his wall
joins another, a corner that enclosed him.

Bucket in hand, he knelt, facing into the angle,
dwarfed by his labour, attending to the end.
With a prayer the mortar sets before it rains,

he slowly disappeared, among the stones.

16.5.2020

I think the Police may be bored

Not a lot happens down our lane.
Once some lads tried to steal a
neighbour's classic red Mustang,
and sometimes a bit of passing
vandalism, but it's a sleepy cul de
sac, leading down to the river walk.

In the ten years I've lived here,
peace has largely reigned,
and rarely do we see police.
So imagine my utter surprise,
returning from the local shop
with legal essential provisions,

to find six bobbies, all standing
about at the end of the road,
looking, frankly, rather bored.
I saw no blood, no swag or drugs –
just a single worried hipster cyclist,
dismounted, in the midst of them.

Now it's a cycle track and bikes
do speed in both directions,
and since the Lockdown, there's
many more walkers – no doubt
collisions do happen, or near
collisions, every now and then.

But six bobbies for a single boy
and his bike? It seemed excessive,
even somewhat worrying to me.
I wondered if they're longing for
a little car chase – maybe a stolen
Mustang, over the Forth bridge

away into deepest, darkest Fife,
the blue light flashing, adrenalin high?
I suppose it would be understandable –

we all need a bit of excitement.

    Especially now.

16.5.2020

I video-conference with my Selves

What is there, isn't always, but
avatars.

The online versions selected.
Simulation.

Which has its virtues, no doubt.
In some ways.

No contamination for one thing.
No shared air.

But it isn't actually *live* life.
Though live-ish.

It's the mirror world, and how it
consumes us.

We see ourselves first, always.
Performing.

Reversed, reflected, inflected.
Some troll-self

sitting in the screen's corner
pretending,

who won't leave the room but
interrupts

even the most intelligent of
observations

with some self-reflexive
revelation

that we are not at all
present but

forever in process of transit.
Time-lagged.

A cipher-self emoji-self.
Winking and

saying, you are not there,
we are just

energy, constantly moving
between us.

No wonder I sometimes forget
who I am

in the breath between speech
and silence.

In the flicker of pixels.

16.5.20

I write a letter of resignation to the Future

I want to say, and let me be clear,
I now give up.

I just don't understand you, or why
you're doing this,

what your aim is, your game plan.
If you have one.

Are we all to be reduced to pixels
on tiny screens?

Is touch to be the dirtiest word of all,
breath, demonised?

I don't think I can be party to this.
I dislike sanitiser.

I dislike conferencing from home.
No boundaries.

We all reach a point where we cannot bend.
This is my limit.

I will live in the past, quietly getting dirty.
And as old as I can.

    I am,

    Resigned.

17.5.20

I prepare the Pyre

They become like plague clothes, these poems,
to be destroyed, burned somehow.
Cast out of mind and sight.

Symbols of a time I now desperately need to forget.
And even forget-me-nots have their season –
even their blues burn, then fade.

Hope can heal, but once the healing's done
it's necessary to let it go – when that happens,
you put the wish beyond your reach.

These clothes have served me well.

    Strike the match.

Dear Subscribers

To all the following people, special thanks are due. Those friends who, by their interest in the poems, have helped to make this book – and in donating to the new press, which is founded on the publication of *Plague Clothes*, those who now help to give birth to a future beyond Covid-19. The gift of friendship and love during Lockdown was great, and now we pay some of that love forward.

RAJ 5.6.2020

Aðalsteinn Ásberg Sigurðsson, Reykjavik; Aileen Ballantyne, Edinburgh; Alex Howard, Edinburgh; Alex Penland, Washington DC & Edinburgh; Alison Craig, Kilbirnie, Ayrshire; Alycia Pirmohammed, Calgary & Edinburgh; Andy Diagram, Newham, London; Andy Duncan, Cupar, Fife; Andy Law, Heriot Toun; Angelo Castiglioni, Edinburgh; Anita Clipston, Manhattan, NYC; Anne Artymiuk, Orkney; Anne Dickie, Zanzibar; Anne Macdonald, Shetland; Anne Sinclair, Fair Isle; Barbara Ziehm, Isle of Lewis; Bella Caledonia; Bernadette Jameson, Ireland; Bhavika Govil, Delhi & Edinburgh; Bjørg Elisabeth Thorn, Lerwick; Brian Holton, Melrose; Brian Smith, Shetland; Byron & Sheila Anderson, Little Fort, British Columbia; Calvin Wharton, North Vancouver, Canada; Camille Manfredi, Daoulas, Brittany; Carla Sassi, between Italy & Scotland; Carol McKay, Hamilton; Catherine Emslie, Meal, Burra, Shetland; Catherine McDonald, Edinburgh; Catherine McInerney, County Down; Catriona MacLellan Smith; Celia Buchan, Scotland; Chelsea Welsh, Edinburgh; Chelsey Beeson, Louisville, Kentucky; Chris Adie, Oban; Chris Agee, Belfast; Chris Powici, Dunblane; Christie Williamson, Partick; Christina Egerstrom, Gothenburg, Sweden;

Craig Bates, Nottingham; Dale Smith, Sandwick, Shetland; Danai Daska, Athens, Greece; David Scott, Cornwall; Deborah Nolan, Hoi An, Vietnam; déirdre ní mhathúna, Edinburgh; Derick Tulloch, Broadside, by Denny; Dexter Yim, Hong Kong; Dima Alzayat, Manchester; Donald Anderson, Waas, Shetland; Donald S Murray, Ness & Shetland; Donna Heddle, Kirkwall, Orkney; Dorothy Lawrenson, Edinburgh; Dorothy McMillan, Glasgow; Duncan McLean, Orkney; Eleanor & Lena Jamieson-Chang; Elizabeth Edwards, Shetland; Emilia Stars, Toronto, Canada; Emma Sedlak, Sydney, Australia; Finola Scott, Glasgow; Fiona Barr Read, Indre et Loire, France; Fiona-Jane Brown, Aberdeen; Francesc Parcerisas, Catalonia; George Gunn, Thurso; Gerald Mangan, Glasgow; Gillian Beattie-Smith, Scottish Borders; Grace & Iain Macniven, Arisaig; Grace Mangan, Edinburgh; Gracie Levack; Greg Walker, Edinburgh; Gwendolyn Enstam, Edinburgh; Hannah Nicolson, Aberdeen; Hanne Tange, Aarhus, Denmark; Hazel & Dmytro, Northern Hemisphere; Hazel B Anderson, Bressay, Shetland; Heather Dawn Ferguson, Dalkeith, Midlothian; Helen Bowell, Scarborough, N Yorks; Hester Levack, Callander; Hester Ross, Edinburgh & Islay; Hugh Kerr, Edinburgh; Hugh McMillan, Penpont; Ian Stephen, Vatisker, Isle of Lewis; Ingibjörg Águstsdóttir, Reykjavik, Iceland; Ingri Johnson, Scatness, Shetland; Irina Nedelcu, London; Iona Ismita Zawinski, Leith; Iris Sandison, Waas, Shetland; Irish Pages; Isabel Sinclair, Shetland; Issie MacPhail, Assynt; Jack & Yumiko Jamieson, Doha, Qatar; James McPherson, Edinburgh; James Oliver, Birrarangga & An t-Eilean Sgitheanach; James Robertson, Newtyle; Jane Harris, East Sussex; Jane Mellor, Vancouver, B.C.; Jane Irina McKie, Linlithgow; Janet De Vigne, Edinburgh; Jean Urquhart, Shetland; Jen Hadfield, Burra, Shetland; Jenny Davidson, New York, NY, USA; Jethro Soutar, Lisbon, Portugal; Jim Benstead, Burgess Hill; Jo Dubé, Peebles; Joan Michael, Ullapool; Joanna Lilley,

Whitehorse, Yukon; Joanne Flaws Jamieson, Shetland; John Cairns, Inverness; John Corbett, Piracaia, Brazil; John Cumming, Orkney; Jonathan Swale, Shetland; Josh Wagner, Nowhere in Particular; Judith Taylor, Aberdeen; Julia Boll, Konstanz, Germany; Kareen Hunter, Shetland; Karen Dawson, Musselburgh; Karina Dent, Scotland; Karina Townsend, Newham, London; Kate Tregaskis, Edinburgh; Katherine Lockton, London; Kathy Hubbard, Wester Quarff, Shetland; Kevin MacNeil, Isle of Lewis & Stirling; Kristin Pedroja, Edinburgh; Laura Di Sciasco, Trieste, Italy; Laura Hird, Edinburgh; Laura McKee, Bexleyheath; Leela Soma, Milngavie, Glasgow; Leith Davis, Vancouver, B.C.; Lena Kraus, River Fowey; Lesley McDowell, Glasgow; Leslie Grollman, between the USA & the Future; Linda Crosfield, Ootischenia B.C.; Lindy Barbour, Ampherlaw, Lanarkshire; Lisa Rigby, Edinburgh; Liz Beer, Ullapool; Liz M & David Miller, St Andrews; Lori Sheirich, Monterey, California; Lorna J. Waite, Edinburgh; Maggie Graham, Glasgow; Maoilios Caimbeul, Isle of Skye; Margaret Roberts, Ollaberry, Shetland; Marina Dossena, Bergamo; Mark Flanagan, NY & Edinburgh; Marsali Taylor, Aith, Shetland; Mary Blance, Lerwick, Shetland; Mary Wight, Melrose; Maxwell Macleod, Cramond Brig; Mike Small, Edinburgh; Miriam Huxley, Edinburgh; Morag McGill, Orkney; Murdo Macdonald, Stornoway, Isle of Lewis; Myranda Jane Bolstad, Yellowknife, NWT, Canada; Nathan Watson, Cornwall & Edinburgh; Neill Walker, South Queensferry; Neville Singh, Edinburgh; Ning Cai, Singapore, UK, Switzerland; Oddfriður Marni Rasmussen, Faroe Islands; Orla Broderick, Hillfoots, Stirling; Pam Celli, Inverness; Pam Perkins, Winnipeg; Pat Law, Heriot Toun; Paul Manson, Abu Dhabi, Aberdeenshire & Lerwick; Rachael McGill, Lisbon, Portugal; Rachel Jupp, Monmouth; Rachel Rankin, Edinburgh; Rasa Ruseckiene, Vilnius, Lithuania; Raymond Smith, Lerwick, Shetland; Robin Gillanders, Edinburgh; Roseanne

Watt, Shetland & Edinburgh; Rosemary Pearson, Westerham, Kent; Roxanne Paris Barker, Denver, Colorado; Ruth Dawkins, Hobart, Tasmania; S M Hutton, New York State, USA; Sally Evans, Callander; Sarah Dunnigan, Edinburgh; Sarah Gull, Bury St Edmunds, Suffolk; Sarah Jane Gibbon, Orphir, Orkney; Sarah McNaughton, Hurricane, West Virginia; Sheila Duncan, Kirkcaldy; Sheila Robertson, Lerwick, Shetland; Silvia Mergenthal, Konstanz, Germany; Simon Manfield, Todmorden; Simon W. Hall, Evie, Orkney; Spencer Thompson, Portland, Oregon; Stuart A Paterson, Galloway; Stuart Swanston, Sciennes, Edinburgh; Sudeep Sen, India; Sue Bryant-Sharples, Cramond Brig; Sue Taylor, Orkney; Suria Tei, Glasgow; Tell it Slant, Glasgow; The Punch, India; Tim Niel, Glasgow; Tom Sharpe, Cramond Brig; Tricia Child, Halifax, W Yorks; Urd Johannesen, Argir, Faroe Islands; Val Mcilreavy, Law; Vicky Tylsar, Shetland; Wendelin Law, Hong Kong; Wendy Leslie, Sidney, B.C.; Wilma Jamieson, Edinburgh; Yvonne Gray, Orkney; Yvonne Wallace, Dunfermline; Zack Abrams, Edinburgh.